A Dance With Fire

Sébastien Streit

A Dance With Fire
By **Sébastien Streit**
Copyright © 2023 Sébastien Streit

ISBN: 978-1-927848-99-9 (Soft Cover)

Filidh Publishing Corp.,

Victoria, BC, Canada

Cover illustration: Laurent Rajotte.

Back cover design by Danny Weeds..

This work is dedicated to

Those whose vision is

Clouded by pain,

Anger, and

Hate.

Love

Will cleanse

Our tumultuous souls

Which dance between states

Of sadness and pure ecstasy.

A Dance With Fire | Sébastien Streit

1.

I played with fire; my hands were burned.
I danced in pain; my world was turned.
A thousand voices did cry out.
Of what they spoke, I have my doubts.

The fire, gone, I yearn for the flame.
I miss the warmth, so hard to tame.
My searing body left alone
To feel the cold amongst my bones.

2.

Obsessed with perfection
I make my confession
And hope it will resolve.

I made the connection
To wound the regression
And hope it will dissolve.

I strive for correction
To slay my oppression
And hope it will depart.

I yearn for affection:
A chance for expression
And hope to share my heart.

3.

A gentle breeze nudging one to the west
Sparks a lust for adventure and freedom
To explore the plains where the rains do rest
And walk each path in the forest's kingdom.

The daunting hills and the lonely mountain
May dissuade travelers from certain routes,
But ever hidden is nature's fountain
And rarely found is the sweetest of fruits.

The roaring rivers are a guide to peace
As they tie the earth together with life,
But even the singing gulls hold a lease
In this temperate world so full of strife.

Yet worry not, my friend, for what will be
And join me in my longing for the sea.

4.

The field so vast, I seek a rose
To fill my soul with song and verse.
With wind to listen to my woes
The field so vast, I seek a rose.
My gaze will blur as I compose
And in its beauty, I immerse.
The field so vast, I seek a rose
To fill my heart with song and verse.

5.

Oh, how the waves of motivation wane
At sight of the unforeseen temptations;
Striking doubt into even the truly sane,
Struggling in their self-emancipation.

A new day brings overwhelming desire
Which can spoil quickly at the turn of a card.
Each moment another goal burns to the fire
Of the fleeting inspiration I discard.

But with disappointment comes new lessons
At which I take no heed to swiftly learn.
For honesty comes from my confessions;
And if nothing is done the problems will return.

The fuel from inspiration may seem fit
But consistency comes only with grit.

6.

Searching inside for the smallest of flaws
May spark in one inspiration for change.
The mere willingness for is worth applause
But effort is needed to rearrange.

How selfishness has burnt many a bridge
On which I may have been able to cross,
Leaving me nothing but a narrow ridge
On which to stand, grieving every loss.

The act of giving was so elusive
In my past as all I knew was to take.
Thoughts of feeding my greed; so intrusive.
I'd drink from an egotistical lake.

But now I can offer my hand to thee
To do with what you want and set me free.

7.

A new opportunity presented
To me excites the inner child within.
So many a path has my mind invented
But the one I walked was one of sin.

Now, the jungle's vines have been untangled
And clear are the murky waters of thought.
Recovered from the scraps; I was mangled
Beyond recognition, fully distraught.

Yet come to my senses have I of late
For only of guidance do I pray now.
Gracefully given a newly cleaned slate
Grants me strength in the yoke to pull the lough.

Alongside whom gives nothing but love;
Grateful am I to be watched from above.

8.

A strict rhyme and a ten-syllable count
Along with a classic meter of old
Makes a verse prance like a king's trusted mount,
Trotting through the streets while glimmering gold.

And the choice of words is choosing a sword
To wield against our foes; darkest of thoughts.
The ringing of steel in the fray may ward
Off the fearful who inside are truly distraught.

A structure, the formation of a battalion
Holds together the thematic meaning
Of a knight riding with his great stallion
Singing as he slays with aura gleaming.

Do not fear restriction in your work
For when applied well you may grow a smirk.

9.

An inquiry made to oneself; a thought,
Of sorts, arises from an inner urge
To connect. Acceptance, eagerly sought,
Enlivens the spirit; a cleansing purge

That swiftly carries imagination
Over into the realm of the unknown
Where everything deserves an exclamation!
I meditate in the sunlight alone.

This query is meant for the curious ears
For if kept to myself I'd be dreaming
Of what couldn't be of my simple fears;
The loved one for whom I've been scheming.

The answer, hidden in a shroud of doubt
Intensifies with my romantic drought.

10.

So ignorant, the infant learns to crawl
In a world so ripe with hatred and spite.
The time is nigh, for death shall take us all.

Life does, to the youthful, seem to enthrall
But know they not of the reapers swift bite?
So ignorant, the infant learns to crawl.

When potent love unto us does befall
So quick is it stripped by relentless blight.
The time is nigh, for death shall take us all.

Even the mightiest will have their fall
As they lose their grip that was once so tight.
So ignorant, the infant learns to crawl.

The few who find the truth will sit and bawl,
Enveloped in an overwhelming fright.
The time is nigh, for death shall take us a ll.

Listen, the beauty of the siren's call
Does inside of me a new flame ignite.
So ignorant, the infant learns to crawl.
The time is nigh, for death shall take us all.

11.

Instead of wasting time, I'll sit and paint
My forming thoughts which haunt my daily dreams.
An image clearly formed, each stroke I taint
The vivid scene of intertwining streams.

Colours so hideous, I'm drawn away
And I forget my weary burning soul.
Dueling myself and I, I wish to stay
A while longer in this lone empty hole.

Soon, hours have passed away, I sit and think
What could have been without my shaking hands.
I stare with sunken eyes thus further I sink.
Elusive were the oils at my command.

Finished! I set my brushes swiftly back
Awaiting the voices relentless attack.

12.

My love seems to hide in the shadows
Where the rays of my sight can't reach.
Searching, I wade through the shallows
As I venture along this beach.

Waves crash to the beat of my heart.
My soul reflects the ocean blue.
Not even the most stunning art
Could draw my eyes away from you.

You, whom I still have yet to see
Somewhere amidst the shifting sands,
So beautiful, I shan't believe
The tales told in the distant lands.

On this path I'll walk to the end
And when we greet, I'll call you friend.

13.

Ride the wave that brings you to shore
Or you'll lose yourself inside the currents.
Who knows of what we have in store?
Who cares? We're doomed to repent.

Clad in shining armour of old,
The child sees nothing but sorrow.
A love for all that isn't gold,
The youth will not hear the morrow.

Oh child, smile and look to the sun
For answers will lead to questions
Of which preface not a page of fun,
But instead--true destruction.

Alas, do you have time to wade
In the water so unafraid?

14.

Thy radiant beauty has lit a flame
In my lonesome heart which aches for one's hand.
A burning impulse too potent to tame
Does heat the iron, so ready to brand.

As the setting sun disappears from view
Embers still glow with thought of their presence,
Warming the fading hope which falls askew
In a dim world devoid of love's essence.

From a spark does the passion rekindle
As dawn does break over the mountain's peak.
The doubts left from the darkness can dwindle,
And immerse do I in your new mystique.

Yet, unattainable is my desire.
So, burn will I in unrelenting fire.

15.

Shall I compare thee to a gentle song?
Sung by the lapping waves atop the shore,
Inspiring passing birds to sing along
Which share the melody that I adore.

Moving so freely with the drifting tide
As setting suns ravage the lustrous earth;
A cycle of beauty that won't subside;
Constant and infinite, a source of mirth.

Dissonance creates a building tension
As the intricate harmony evolves.
Complexity demands true attention
Until nature's cacophony resolves.

So long as the sounds by the sea persist,
Here, no great perfection will exist.

16.

To unearth the rose from the field
Would prove corruption from my greed.
Deep in mind a well rooted weed;
To unearth the rose from the field.
Against instinct, I need a shield
For evil thoughts do I conceded.
To unearth the rose from the field
Would prove corruption from my greed.

17.

Why do I try to lend my heart
To those whom which my eyes find fair?
When without fail we fall apart
Too premature for them to care.

And countless attempts at romance
Leave the word as a bitter taste
As even with my closest chance
Lust seems to disappear in haste.

Still yearning for a hand to hold
While walking down a rocky beach
I'm waiting for love to unfold
And gently fall within my reach.

Shall I exhaust myself in chase
Or learn to love myself in place?

18.

The tranquility of the breaking dawn
Long before my friends wake from gentle sleep
Sparks self-reflection of my past forgone
And rids me of the tears I used to weep.

The little lapping waves against the shore
And the rustling of the wind through the leaves
Are subtle sounds my heart does so adore
For beauty mother nature softly weaves.

The dancing flowers in the waving grass
Bring colour to this wide and open field.
The rising sun carries life, time does pass,
Feeling free, oh how glad I am to be!

19.

Where mountains are white, oceans are blue,
My heart knows never what to do.
Where rivers flow and trees are full
I'm tempted by this graceful pull.
Will I be left full of remorse
If I should choose the quicker course
Past rolling hills and crystal watered streams,
Missing out on my wildest of dreams.
Do I turn left, right, or go back
Or stand so still and choose not to act?

20.

Do the shedding trees miss their falling leaves?
Should one accept the nature of their loss?
I know not as I am one who still grieves
The moment time froze as you walked across.

Naked and bare, the wind strips them of hope
As the fading sunlight offers no love.
How do these solitary beings cope?
Do they too believe in something above?

Come spring their leaves return by the plenty.
Yet still am I, a wanderer, on my own
Cursed by my love. My heart will stay empty
As my envy mounts while I'm alone.

Should one mimic the stoic stance of trees
Or spoil away by jealous disease?

21.

We danced together on solid ground.
I thought we'd forever resist the fall.
Then all the music stopped and my feet found
The hidden truth at the base of the wall.

A wall you had built, without my consent,
Now casts tall shadows on my world of light.
And in the shade, a hazed over descent,
Blinded by darkness, brought relentless fright.

Without my knowledge you had tied my hands
With ropes of a colour I could not recall.
You said you'd take me to magical lands
If I'd dismiss my dislike of your wall.

My thoughts escaped; observing their ascent
I spread the fire to cast away the night.
Oh, how did I let such ripe fruit ferment
I missed my chance at tasting their delight.

22.

How one may wish to dance with me
Does seem far-fetched; a lonesome soul.
So deeply rooted is this tree;
How one may wish to dance with me.
The fallen yearn for love from thee
And lack the gift of feeling whole.
How one may wish to dance with me
Does seem far-fetched; a lonesome soul.

23.

I sit impatiently.
Where eyes used to wander.
I watch fellow sheep graze
The meadows of knowledge,
So stimulated yet skillfully unaware
Of their dependence on accessibility.
What would they do if we lost electricity?
Would the dry weeds of our stale present
Satisfy such thirsty beasts?
Or would their palates still crave
The sweet disconnected feast.

24.

The wrong key in my pocket, all along,
Granted me luck to have made it this far.
Arrived at this door I was headstrong,
Without a clue of breaking it ajar.

While locks I've seen many, this one stood out,
Much like a black sheep hiding in plain view.
My brass friend could not help, I was left to pout
And whine and cry for I knew that it was true.

Seasons pass by and still I sit alone.
To think patience grants exceptions for me
Makes a fool of myself for that is known.
And spoiled am I, believing I'm free.

To hell with opening this stupid gate.
I have no more time to sit here and wait.

25.

To let fear guide one's hand is to succumb
Willingly to suffering a lost path.
Where hidden denial gracefully numbs
Any insight to rid oneself of wrath.

So naturally can worry dissuade
One to give up their determination.
Of failure does one find themselves afraid
Once blighted by swift degradation.

Having walked a path of my own desire
Led only by my delusional thought
I saw an inextinguishable fire
Forever leaving my mind distraught.

The screaming banshee burnt into my soul
A fear so great that I'd lose my control.

26.

The day isn't going as planned.
My demons swim about,
They murmur, scream, and shout
At me, turning my feet to sand.

Sinking in absolute silence,
Dancing with the devil,
A rare chance to revel
Alone, and take in my sentence.

Reflecting hinders the flow of life.
Put a damper on thought,
Sit back and pluck the taut
Six strings, letting go of your strife.

My day isn't going as planned.
I guess I'll just enjoy the sand.

27.

Such jealousy has arisen in me,
Clouding my judgment and obscuring my thought,
That when I cast my gaze upon the sea
I see clearly my efforts all for naught.

A gaze that could find joy in any light
And recognize the rights from many wrongs
Offers sight of beauty hidden from plain sight
Blurring the envy's convincing song.

But how does one release these clutching jaws
Which dig deeply into my fleeting will,
Relentlessly testing my strength without pause.
I find an escape with parchment and quill.

My yearning for love has ignited a flame
Thus bringing to me a beast to tame.

28.

It feels as if the world lacks faith in me
To dance amongst the flowering daffodils
Or sing along with robins flying free;
For they seem lost about the hills.

But faith do I hold so close to my heart
That I shall continue to push on through
Until turmoil and pain from me depart
And the world takes on a colourful hue.

For not all wanderers find themselves lost
In this world where harsh expectations reigns.
But where will I end up and at what cost?
How much bleach need I to cleanse my stains.

One step forward, two steps back, all in spite,
I will trudge my way on and win this fight.

29.

How grateful I've become to those around
Whom share their love for me, with me: my friends.
And family too whose caring voices sound
A warming tone my heart can comprehend.

Yet still my selfish nature asks for more
More love, more praise, more chances to be heard.
As seldom do I get to stand before
A person to whom my past isn't blurred.

For honesty I practice day to day,
One day at a time, the forgotten lies
Will clear and with my true self on display
I'll stare into your bright and starry eyes.

The words I yearn to hear from you, a plead,
Are "would you like to spend some time with me?"

30.

To visit old friends is to bring warmth straight
Into my heart; a soft and gentle embrace
Which comforts me so and removes the weight
Of the world allowing entry of grace.

Worries vanish as our eyes lock in trust
Or are discussed until the early morn.
Where a helping hand will shake off the rust
Maybe sing some songs of roses and thorns.

Laughing amongst those closest to me
Brings but joyous sentiment to my heart.
How fear subsides and my stresses depart;
Insecurities leave and I feel whole.

What did I do to deserve such great friends?
The love I share with them shan't never end.

31.

A wanderer on route to the city of ash,
Leaning atop his trusted staff,
Wades through the murky waters of thought,
A ponderer by nature, through internal wars fought.
So weary, his mind was distraught.
His very soul, so brutally wrought,
Led to his fall. Before his eyes a flash
Presents a scene; his other half.

A fork in the road, a choice on his path;
Disgusted, he leaves in wrath.

32.

What is so beautiful about a rose?
Like all other flowers it will wilt
And in time will come to a close.
Its marred petals, a displayed guilt,
Now bestowed upon the silt.
What is so beautiful about a rose?

33.

Tell me why I shouldn't play with fire again.
For its warmth, so inviting, welcomes me
More than any friend I could attain.
So cunning is the flame; I hear its plea.

But danced have I, here, on this ground before,
Where nothing but my pain could have been felt.
And all the energy I had in store
Was used to accept the cards that I'd been dealt.

I know the outcome. I've seen the result.
Yet part of me, a subtle part, still yearns
To kiss the fire before I can consult
With myself. I guess this child never learns.

So hot to the touch I snap my hand back
Away from the flame, evading the attack.

34.

Rivers lit with gold fade to black
And I worry for my friend
Who still travels a lost track
With skills to succeed he surely lacks.

Trees of white trouble him not
As his eyes are fixed on the end.
Light peaks over the hill, he's caught.
Hope re-found he switches to a trot.

Now he gallops, kick up dust,
Storming forth, as he must.

35.

Lost am I, for the world's expectations
Baffle me and leave me in confusion.
A pearl in the sea; what revelations
Arise, adding to my dissolution.

As I dance and flout through whims of courage
I dig myself a deeper hole to climb.
Here and there my consistent pilferage
Of knowledge doesn't stop the passing time.

Now further down this path of disarray
I find myself imbued with fiery desire
To change my tactics; this chaotic fray
Where everything I touch turns to fire.

I seek a spring whose water's ever clear
And pray for guidance and removal from fear.

36.

To write in pencil or pen
Decides everything.
Either live with one's mistakes
Or sacrifice spontaneity.
To capture the moment in truth
Requires a steady hand and ink.
But one can develop a thought
With patience and a second chance.

37.

What's left behind flutters free in my chest
Like dying butterflies hiding in my heart.
Thorough thoughts paint a sorrowful crest
Which I cast away as abdicable art.

The road ahead will dance without a doubt
And sing will I to push my demons away.
Of what I seek I know nothing about;
Walking, running, falling, ever more astray.

Stay back foul beast for I forbid thy thought
From tempting me with thy fraudulent lust.
Now venture forth for thy hatred shall rot.
And when you return, I'll curse you to rust.

I step on you and free myself of guilt
And watch my shifting view of beauty tilt.

38.

The night engulfs my peaceful thoughts
As water consumed Atlantis.
A small, burning, decrepit spot,
The ember of my searing bliss:

A kiss from the sun. And they're gone!
Quicker than froth on sandy shores.
Light fuels the birth of a new dawn,
Whose life begins with no closed doors.

39.

Lost is the world for my expectations
Taint the beauty freely offered to me.
How disillusioned are my frustrations
Where necessities, obscured, are hard to see.

The simplicity I seek in my life
Is hidden in a shroud of the thickest fog
Where all my efforts lead only to strife.
Oh, how I hope this is but the prologue.

Pure curiosity will never spoil
But I have yet to find what stokes the flames
Of passion which even through my turmoil
Will keep the burning embers hot in my veins.

I may be one who is cursed to wander
But am I lost traveling over yonder?

40.

A void in my friendships tears me apart
For my actions blinded me from the truth.
Unaware, I found a pain in my heart.
Am I alone in enjoying my youth?

I smile and joke and don't mean any harm
But there's the odd person I seem to hurt.
Have I lost my innate caring and charm?
Or do I feast on pain as one does dessert?

Reflected, have I, on what could improve
This quick parting of the land and the sea.
Slowly do the delicate saplings prove
Their place in the forest amongst the trees.

Listen up, listen now, and listen here!
There's a new ecstatic me drawing near.

41.

An uncontrollable reaction
As my thoughts spiraled in abstraction
Created a scene of unease.
I beg you to listen, please.

I do not judge one's past
And what I know isn't vast
But my emotions I couldn't suppress
As my heart beat against my chest.

I apologize if I scared you
As my personality changed its hue.
I must have appeared as a maniac
As I dealt with an abrupt attack.

Not from what you shared,
But I admit I was not prepared.
I think it stemmed from stress
And some past experience's mess.

Please know I'm not running away
From what you tried to convey
For I still would like to have some tea
And maybe share a bit about me.

42.

As rain batters atop the earth
The grasses dance, the flowers bloom
And birds sing in contagious mirth
As rain batters atop the earth.
Winds bring news of joyous rebirth;
The lifting of our winter's gloom.
As rain batters atop the earth
The grasses dance, the flowers bloom.

43.

The puzzle of making syllables match
While hiding my thoughts for the keen to catch
And searching for rhymes however diverse,
Oh, the joy of writing in verse!

But never neglecting rhythm or flow
Of what I speak even I do not know.
If I can't fit a word I swear and curse,
Oh, the joy of writing in verse!

At home or at work or while taking a stroll
The words on paper are in my control.
Without or with pen, my thoughts rehearse,
Oh, the joy of writing in verse!

Through limerick or sonnet or villanelle
I can feel my mind fall into a spell.
In my black notebook, so small, I immerse.
Oh, the joy of writing in verse.

44.

The falling snowflakes kiss your rosy cheeks
Uncovered by your scarf of woven wool.
The sun glints off the snowy mountain peaks
Like the joy in your eyes that gently pull

Me towards your lovingly soft embrace;
Blanketing me in a comfort so true.
Your floral perfume as we interlace
Excites my mind for what just might ensue.

As you start to loosen your gentle hold
The wisping wind does freely fly between
Our silhouettes, who standing in the cold,
Do seem still as painted figurines.

I sit so near the woodstove burning bright
Dreaming of when I'll be your shining knight.

45.

Amongst the rocks there laid some gems.
Bright and shining they caught my eye.
I asked of where such beauty stems;
To my luck there was no reply.

Onwards I ventured down the beach
Listening to the seagulls sing.
The water's edge was within reach
But suddenly my soul did sting.

The driftwood drifting on the waves
And the soothing sounds of the sea
Remind my heart of how it craves
For a gentle embrace from thee.

But you know not of how I feel,
For I know not if you are real.

46.

Let your worries wash away.
Floating down the river
Is where troubles should stay.

Watch them drift by, untouched
While you stand and quiver
With joy, stress uncluctched.

Smile! They're taken from sight
Your soul shines like silver,
Reflecting the bright light.

Soon, a thought, here to play,
Forces you to shiver.
Let your worries wash away.

47.

Behind the weeping willow's veil
Enclosed, where all the sunlight fails
There stood a figure, hunched and frail
Lost amidst the tangled trails.

Whence it came none can recall
But surely from outside the walls.
At dawn it wakes and starts to crawl
By dusk it cries and swiftly falls.

The passerby will turn his gaze
And children many questions raise.
Lying there in dirt it stays
And watches with its eyes ablaze.

For all it knows is hate and pain
And anger, anguish, such disdain.
But how it feels it can't explain
And thus it rots in its domain.

48.

So many a flower has grown since
Our hands were locked and eternally bound.
Do you recall of your forgotten prince
Who shared with you his heart so rarely found?

The glimmer of your brightly hazeled eyes
And the shimmer of your lost but golden hair
Still vivid in my mind, a perfect guise
Which all who lay their prying eyes find fair.

But fairer yet, just as an angel sings
Of brilliant joy and heavenly light,
Your voice, or memory of, gently brings
Me back to days when passion did ignite

A love so fiery that flames would sear
Yearning in me in hopes you'd reappear.

49.

A soft touch accompanied by laughter
Warms my heart, nurturing my desire
For a hand to hold now and hereafter;
So elusive has love been to acquire.

Comfort from her smile and her soothing voice
As I vulnerably share my past
Fosters trust, of which I lack, so I rejoice
For surely gone is the doubt that had amassed.

Forgotten had I of the blinding joy -
The flash in the sky that strikes through the heart -
That humbles me, a man fearful and coy
Whose every chance at love did swiftly depart.

To live in kindness and to live with grace
Outpace the ones trying to win the race.

50.

While part of me will grieve and yearn
The other stands tall and proud
For I may bend as I grow stern
But break I won't or call me loud!

I bid farewell - thorn in my side -
Crutch! I name thee; stolen have you
From the waters of love's own tide,
Crystal clear turquoise: shades of blue.

Blue like the eyes of my thief.
That lying rat! Coins to his name
He had none - yet to his belief -
He was steps ahead of the game.

Alas, vanished has he for good;
The scoundrel who spoiled my soul
That decadent liar who could
And would cheat me into a hole.

Acknowledgments

I would like to thank my parents, first and foremost, Christian and Kelly, for all the love and support they have offered me throughout my life.

Monet, thank you for being who you are and inspiring me with your passion for loving and appreciating all which falls in your path.

Thank you, Mike, for all the great support over the last few years. I always look forward to hearing great advice from you.

Zoe, thank you for working with me yet again and helping me get my work out to the public.

Jo-Anne, thank you for once again sifting through my work and finding my many inconsistencies. I've learned so much from reading the suggestions you offer.

About the Author

Sébastien passionately pursues many creative outlets in his spare time. Poetry is a form of expression which he has become quite attached to. As a cathartic release, it has helped him through the plethora of emotions a person confronts on a daily basis.

Having always loved playing with words, it is only natural that he finds himself writing in verse. He believes there are many ways to enjoy a poem. Reading it silently in one's head, reading it aloud, and, best of all, having someone else read it aloud.

Sébastien hopes everyone can gain something from reading his work and encourages any sort of feedback.

www.ingramcontent.com/pod-product-compliance
Lightning Source LLC
Chambersburg PA
CBHW022125040426
42450CB00006B/854